8/6/05

MW01250957

My classmate, Mary
Be Blessed &
Enjoy the book

Whatever Floats Your Boat

Love Ya

[signature]

Whatever Floats Your Boat

Donna Fareed (Warfield)

iUniverse, Inc.
New York Lincoln Shanghai

Whatever Floats Your Boat

iUniverse books may be ordered through booksellers or by contacting:

iUniverse
2021 Pine Lake Road, Suite 100
Lincoln, NE 68512
www.iuniverse.com
1-800-Authors (1-800-288-4677)

ISBN: 0-595-34203-5

Printed in the United States of America

Table of Contents

FOREWORD

This writing is dedicated to the following people who have been instrumental in my life in different ways:

Vern and Mary Frances Warfield, my parents

The late Dr. William Caesar Warfield, my Uncle

Patrick Warfield, Virginia Warfield, Charles Warfield and Doreen Warfield Graney, my siblings

Beverly Coleman, my dearest and best girl friend

This writing is also dedicated to everyone who has sat under my teachings and to all those whom I have had the privilege of inspiring and motivating through speaking engagements, seminars and workshops.

And,

Last, but in no way least, I must say thank you to the love of my life, my best friend, confidant, my biggest supporter, the person who challenges me the most and loves me in spite of my shortcomings and imperfections: my husband, Mel Fareed.

This writing has been directed by the spirit of my higher being. It is through revelation and knowledge of his truth that I am able to bring forth this work. I have been given authority and a mandate to release this book into the marketplace, to touch all walks of life. This is a mandate I don't take lightly. May the words of this book enlighten you and leave you with peace, inner prosperity, fulfillment and victory.

INTRODUCTION

What floats your boat? In other words, what drives you? What motivates you? What keeps you going? What inspires you? What encourages you to keep moving? What makes you happy? What makes you content? What brings you joy? What satisfies you? What turns you on? What keeps that fire for life within you burning?

Does money float your boat? Do your children float your boat? Do your affiliations float your boat? Do YOU float your boat? Does your education float your boat? Does your economic status float your boat? Does your position in the work place float your boat? Does your employer float your boat? Does success float your boat? Does your spouse float your boat?

I have not earned a doctorate degree yet. I am not a psychologist or a psychiatrist. I am a woman who has a love for people who has had her share of victories and defeats. My sole purpose is to see others set free—delivered from themselves and each other and liberated from everything that results in defeat.

Over the years I have opened and closed chapters in my life, which have become a book of memoirs and experiences. This best-selling book has been bottled up in my heart, but you have not been privy to it. It has been written on the tablet of my heart and for the first time I have a burden to release it. There is an old familiar saying that states, "We learn by experience." That may be true in some instances, but I've come to a place in my life where I don't necessarily have to learn by experience. The wise person knows when to learn from others experiences and avoid unnecessary pain. Experience can sometimes be a hard teacher; you get the test first and then you learn the lesson. For those of you who have not experienced much pain, my desire is that you would embrace this reading and not have to go through some of the pain that others or I have gone through. For those of you who are experiencing pain I trust that you find your way out of it. I have run across many people who have never fully recovered from adverse situations or encounters. Experience is not always the best teacher.

The purpose of this writing is not to beat you up or to criticize, but to encourage you to effectively move forward in your life. I have known many well-meaning people whose approach to helping others was not effective because of how help was delivered or presented. I trust the presentation of this writing will not offend but will encourage, motivate and inspire you to move forward in a positive fashion. This book was written to get right to the point. As a result, I hope it will be clear and concise to you, the reader. I also hope it will trigger you to think and look at where you are, and most importantly, what you can do to enhance yourself and move forward. Some of you may read this book in one sitting, while others may take more time. You may have to stop and take a "think break" and then resume. Whatever your style of reading, I trust that you will find value in this writing.

Prior to reading this book, clear your mind so that you are open to receive some life-changing nuggets. If you or someone you know has been down and out, on top of the mountain or in the valley, accused and convicted, forsaken and rejected, perplexed and bewildered, used and abused, tortured and tormented, this book is for you. If you feel weak, lost, confused, misunderstood, unsure or insecure, this book is also for you. If you believe you have it all together, this book is especially for you.

As you read the following chapters, my desire is that you will gain insight into relevant knowledge. I hope this knowledge will prick the very center of your heart, regardless of where you are in life. This writing may cause you to resist, but that is okay; don't be alarmed. Continue to the end. I trust that as you continue the resistance will eventually diminish. You will begin to embrace the writing. As a result, positive changes will come forth in your life. Change can be for your good and choosing not to change can be detrimental. You can choose not to do anything and stay where you are. The decision is yours.

This writing has none of the following barriers:

- Race
- Age
- Gender
- Status
- Politics

• Education

This book is a compilation of thoughts, research and experiences, which will cause you to think, re-examine, re-group and re-focus on what "really" matters. I trust you will be a better person for taking the time to go on this adventuresome sail with me. Please read this book from the beginning to the end. Do not start in the middle or at the end. If you follow the sequential order of the book it will benefit you. This book will motivate you to THINK, it will motivate you to CHANGE and it will bring you to a place of VICTORY in all areas of your life.

We all have the tendency to talk ourselves into failure. It seems for every person I meet who is optimistic; I meet ten who feel afraid and anxious about tomorrow. Perhaps this imbalance is a reflection of the fast-paced, high-pressured environment in which we live. We make up the environment we live in. In other words, the environment is derived from people who live in it. We have chosen to live fast-paced lives, which leads to pressure if we do not know how to "hold" and "fold". Holding and folding simply means to do those things that eliminate stress and anxiety. Have you listened critically to a thirty-minute newscast lately? Forget trying to absorb what is happening, and concentrate on the tone of these broadcasts. We are bombarded with an over-emphasis on losses and limitations, misery and suffering.

There is a saying that states, "The tide always comes back." True to that thought, the tide will come in; the boat will float again and the worn and ugly bottom will be hidden underwater. Certainly, things may be tough today. Your job may be going badly or you may not have a job. Illness may have invaded your family. Debts may be piling up.
We have all been bleached by these low tides in our lives. But wait, be patient. The tide will come back in! You don't have to abandon ship. We have only to plan mentally and spiritually for the tide's return. The person who fails is the one who gives up and surrenders the ship because the tide is out. Sigmund Freud said, "The chief duty of humans is to endure life." The tide may just be turning again for you. Why not be patient and see for yourself before you jump ship.

Now sit back, relax and put on your life jacket and NO JUMPING SHIP. The water may come over the sides and slap you on the face from time to time. You may even feel as though you are going to shipwreck. Whatever you do, stay in the boat until it is time to get off.

Throughout the reading you will see the question mark symbol (**?**). That will let you know a question is on its way. These are thought-provoking questions to get you to think about what is being asked and to allow you time to reflect.

WE ARE ABOUT TO GO ASHORE. LAST CALL TO GET ON BOARD!

ALL ABOARD!

1

"WHATEVER"

There are a number of definitions for the word "whatever". Here's what Webster's Dictionary has to say about it:

1). Of any number or kind.
   Example: "Whatever requests you make will be granted."

2). All of; the whole of.
   Example: "She applied whatever strength she had left to the task."

3). Everything or anything.
   Example: *"Do whatever you please."*

4). No matter what.
   Example: *"Whatever happens, we'll meet here tonight".*

5). What ever.
   Example: *"Whatever does he mean?"*

For the purpose of this book and this specific chapter, allow me to concentrate on the word "whatever" being used in a carefree type of manner. In other words, I am not going to deal with this situation. I am not going to address it. I am going to blow it off or dismiss it.

(?)

Have you ever been in a situation that disturbed you or made you feel uncomfortable? It could have been on the job or at school. Perhaps it involved someone you loved, maybe a spouse, one of your children, a sister or brother, a girlfriend or boyfriend, a cousin, an aunt or uncle, a niece, a nephew or an in-law. It might have been your best friend or someone on your job, a teacher, someone from your church or even your doctor. In that situation, did you choose not to address or confront whatever it was that disturbed you? Did you shrug it off by mentally and/or verbally saying, "whatever"?

Do you fall in that category? Have you ever found yourself in that category? Do you know of others who are in that category? I believe every one of us has fallen into that category at some time in our lives or know of others who often find themselves in that situation. It usually occurs when we have been given correction, constructive criticism or when negative situations occur.

Oftentimes, we chose not to deal with it and shrug it off because deep down we do not want to expose how we feel for fear we might be rejected or humiliated. In some instances, it is too painful to deal with so we'd rather shrug it off by saying, "whatever". The final result fosters an unhealthy state of escapism. Allow me to dig a little deeper.

According to Webster's Dictionary, escapism means:

"The tendency to escape from daily reality or routine by indulging in daydreaming, fantasy, or entertainment."

According to Webster's New World Dictionary of the American Language, escapism means:

"A tendency to escape from reality, responsibilities, etc., especially through the imagination."

There is nothing wrong with imagining as long as you use a "healthy" imagination. However, imagination that takes on the form of escapism is not productive. In the long run, it can hurt you.

Let's dock for a few moments to search our hearts. You never know what may be found.

(?)

Have you ever been in a relationship with someone and that person did something to hurt your feelings or offend you? It could have been a spouse, a sibling, a best friend, a business partner or a co-worker. Think about these other scenarios:

- You have been physically or mentally abused.
- You are accused of doing something you didn't do.
- You are in a position of authority and are suddenly removed.
- You are a member of an organization and you have a disagreement with another member.

Instead of going to the person and confronting the situation, you chose to do one or more of the following:

- Tell someone else what happened and how you feel about it.
- Become angry and separate yourself from the person.
- In a group setting with the person who hurt or offended you, you belligerently throw out little digs.
- You confront the person, but in the wrong way.
- Take the attitude of "whatever" and attempt to forget.

Notice I said attempt. It is a rare person who forgets. We may move on, but rarely do we forget. Typically, when we take the "whatever" attitude, we end up manifesting all or some of the above choices. We end up holding and bottling up our emotions. As a result, it affects us in a negative way. Some of us even go so far as telling the person off in our minds. We imagine ourselves in the person's face, giving them a piece of our mind. Some find comfort in this, but it is only temporary comfort. It may bring peace for a moment, but it won't last because there is no closure. This is an instance where imagination can be harmful. Many times the person who we have a problem with doesn't even know there is a problem. Granted, there are times when we are not able to confront someone face-to-face. Maybe the person is no longer living or cannot be found. In those instances, we can still address it by coming to a place within our hearts where we find peace and no longer take an attitude of "whatever."

In my own life, I have been guilty of confronting or addressing adverse situations in the wrong way. Rather than taking time to cool down and re-think before speaking, I've made matters worse by incorrectly addressing certain situations. Over the years, I've learned how to address these situations. Guess what? I'm still learning. By the way, did I forget to tell you that I am not perfect? I am still learning and growing just like everyone else. I have never met a person who has a degree in everything. Although there are many who will give you that impression. Have you ever run across any of them? Don't rule them out. There is a reason for that type of behavior. We have to learn the art of being patient with others and focus on how we can work together as opposed to fighting against each other.

If our paths ever cross, remind me to tell you my approach to people who know everything. I don't think any of us will ever get to a place in our lives where we have it all together. I believe there will always be something in our character that needs work.

Let me assure you that if you are willing to take the time out to continually develop your character, you will be amazed at the help that is out there.

By addressing our "whatevers," we find ourselves being truthful with our feelings. Knowing the truth will liberate you—not the truth itself, but *knowing* the truth. What does the term "knowing" mean?

The word "know" is a verb, whereas the word "knowing" is an adjective. The adjective "**knowing**" has these four senses:

1. knowing, wise

2. deliberate, intentional, knowing, willful

3. aware, knowing, knowledgeable

4. enlightened, knowing, knowledgeable, learned, lettered, well-educated

Taken from: WordNet 2.0 Vocabulary

Merriam-Webster's Dictionary's definition of knowing is:

1. to have an understanding of

2. to be aware of the truth or factuality

3. to have knowledge

Becoming intimate with the truth or knowing the truth about our own hang-ups, misperceptions and insecurities is the first step to victory. Owning up to them by acknowledging them gets us to that step. We are now aware of what is going on, we have an understanding, we have knowledge and we are wise about the situation. There is an old proverb that states, "…in all thy getting; get an understanding." *(Proverbs 4:7).*

Again, knowing the truth—not the truth itself, but knowing the truth—learning about the truth, running after the truth, looking for the truth, embracing the truth, understanding the truth, seeking the truth will liberate you.

The truth can stand by itself. It needs no one to defend it. We have been fooled into believing that truth does not matter anymore and that as humans, we have the innate ability to define the standard for what is or is not true. We have been given a free will to make our own decisions. Just because we have been given a free will to make our own decisions does not mean there is no standard for truth. There are many schools of thought, ideals and perceptions, but there is only one truth.

When we continue to ignore those areas in our lives where we need help the result is a very confused, misled, perplexed, misunderstood, angry, bitter human being who has often times done a good job of covering up or hiding. We mask ourselves in many ways: by being the life of the party, by excelling in education, by living our lives behind our spouses or children, by joining organizations, even becoming church members and possibly hiding behind money. Those are only a few examples. There are many, many more. This list of hiding places is as long as the imagination.

Allow me to tell you the truth about yourself:

- You are unique
- You can be successful
- You are not a doormat
- You are not a spare tire
- You are not second best
- You have talent and skills

- You have a deep beauty within
- You were wonderfully created
- No one can beat you *being* you
- You are not someone's else ticket to success

Let's get back to addressing our "whatevers". When one addresses those "whatevers," the process of liberating oneself or getting set free begins to take place.

Another familiar quotation is, "…to thine own self be true," from William Shakespeare's *Hamlet:*

The following is the entire quote:

"Neither a borrower nor a lender be; for loan oft loses both itself and friend, and borrowing dulls the edge of husbandry. This above all: to thine own self be true."

In other words be true to yourself. If we are not true to ourselves, how can we be true to others?

Let's relate this to the very first question that was asked: Someone you are in a relationship with hurts or offends you. An approach I've used that seems to work is to ask myself the following questions:

- Am I over-reacting?
- Am I being too sensitive?
- What is behind the hurt or offense?
- This hurts me; why am I hurting or why am I offended?
- Is this person trying to be a friend to me by telling me the truth about myself, even if it hurts?

Once those questions or similar questions have been asked and answered, and you are still having a hard time, it is probably time to go to the person and address it. Through my own experiences, I have found that many times, after I ask myself those questions and took time to address them, I realized that perhaps this is just me—and it isn't an "issue."

If you go to the person and address it the right way, you have freed yourself from being in bondage. I do realize that sometimes there may be fear in approaching a person because you are not sure how you will be received. However, if you go with the right attitude and your motives are right, and still the person does not seem to be receptive; in my opinion it is no longer an issue for you. You've done all you can. I put it in the "PP" category; pray for the person and move on. "PP" stands for "personal problem."

(?)

Has anyone ever gotten on your nerves to the degree that you didn't care what he or she did? You may be experiencing a situation such as this right now. You shrugged your shoulders and said a few choice words and took the attitude of "whatever" or "I don't care". Stop lying to yourself. Remember, "...to thine own self be true." You do care. Come clean with yourself; fess up, stop running and address it correctly.

It appears as though we have hit a current of water so high; it is now splashing you. The force of the water is so strong; it stings your skin. Don't be concerned. It's a beautiful sunny day. You will dry off and be fine.

There is nothing wrong with confrontation as long as it is done correctly. There is a correct way and an incorrect way to confront or address negative situations or encounters. An attitude of "whatever" is not the correct way to confront those situations. Even though we believe we are walking away from it; our feelings don't leave. We allow our feelings to grow in our thoughts and mind, and although we don't verbalize it, we do verbalize it internally. It is not wise to confront a person while angry and hurt. I have found through experience that it is always best to give yourself time before approaching someone. Plain and simple, it's called a "waiting period." Many times we jump out there without giving ourselves time to think, regroup and assess the situation. We then say and do things we might not have—had we waited.

(?)

Think of a situation when something bothered you. Instead of verbalizing your feelings, you held them in. But your feelings began to obviously show in your actions.

For example, someone said something to you that you did not appreciate. You held it in and later that day you were in the presence of the person along with a group of others. You began to jokingly lash out at this person and the group began to laugh. You've allowed what you bottled up to manifest itself negatively through your outburst against this person, whether you did it jokingly or not. Furthermore, it is just another cover up.

Let's close this leg of our cruise as we begin to see shore, understanding that an attitude of "whatever" cannot and will not float your boat or lead you in the direction that you should go. Take note that I did not say in the direction that you want to go. I said in the direction you should go.

When we say "whatever" in the perspective that I have been speaking of, we are really being cowardly and complacent. We are bowing out. That statement may hurt. You may be feeling a splash. You may even want to jump ship, but don't. I feel comfortable making these statements because I've been there. At times in my life, I did not want to address or confront a person due to the following:

- Not sure how it would be received
- Not wanting to embarrass myself by becoming emotional
- Not wanting the person to know that the situation bothered me
- Afraid that the person I addressed would become angry with me

I was once told to embrace the Ban deodorant advertising slogan, "Never let them see you sweat."

Well, I have news for you. You can still confront or address situations and not sweat.

What we say when we decide to take the "whatever" path is, "I don't want to deal with this." Guess what? You are absolutely correct. You don't have to deal with it. Again, it is your choice.

However, deep inside you want to deal with it. A cry deep within says, "This hurts and I am not comfortable." As we suppress these feelings it causes emotional turmoil that can lead to severe damage to your over all well-being. This affects others who are a part of your life.

These suppressions become baggage that we carry as we go through life. After awhile we stop carrying baggage and we have now accumulated trunks that are too heavy to carry, so we pull the trunks on wheels. These trunks weigh us down and hinder us from doing what we were placed on this Earth to do. Are you tired of pulling trunks of hurt, resentment, bitterness, confusion and unresolved issues? Are you tired of pulling other people's trunks? If so, let's sail forward. If not, drift forward with the current anyway.

I trust that the next time you say or take the "whatever" attitude you will regroup and address the situation in the right manner instead of turning away from it. This is critical if you really have a desire for your life to float in the right direction.

2

FLOATING

What comes to your mind when you think of the word "floating?"

Do you think of peace and security or do you think of drowning and turmoil?

According to Webster's Dictionary the definition of the word "float" or "floating" means:

    a.   to remain suspended within or on the surface of a fluid without sinking.

    b.   to be suspended in or move through space as if supported by a liquid.

    c.   to put into the water; launch; *float a ship*; *float a navy*

1). To move from place to place, especially at random.

2). To move easily or lightly.

3). To cause to remain suspended without sinking or falling.

(?)

Do you sometimes feel like a vagabond?

Do you feel as though there is no meaning in your life?

Do you feel as though you are here on Earth, just existing?

Do you find yourself wandering with no purpose or direction?

Do you feel as if you are playing or "acting out" a life that is not your own?

I once had a dream that was absolutely awesome. My life was great in this dream. Everything seemed to be going right. All of a sudden I started sinking. When I began to sink I panicked and became desperate. My awesome dream turned into a nightmare.

Many times we float about in life, never thinking about what we are here on Earth to do. We end up doing things to please others or we end up doing things with the wrong motives. Sometimes we are allowed to float about or remain suspended for quite some time without sinking or falling. Then, all of a sudden, the storms come and we lose our footing. We start making wrong decisions out of desperation. We then try to remedy the situation or simply cope with all the turmoil. Most of us call this survival.

A mistake we often make is not taking time to ask ourselves why this is happening. Perhaps it is happening because it is supposed to happen. Maybe I was going in the wrong direction and perhaps this happened to get me where I need to be. Even though it is a negative situation, it is for my good. I've been floating around all this time thinking this is the life of me. Is this really the life I should be living?

This is a good time to look outside ourselves and look at freshwater species that spend their lifetime floating. As these freshwater fish are introduced to you, take some time to ponder whether any of them remind you of you.

Freshwater fish are flesh of fish from fresh water used as food.
Definition Taken From: Wordnet 1.7.1
Source: Setting Up A Freshwater Aquarium; by Gregory Skomal
(Red Devil, Guppy, Kissing Gourami)

Red Devil—as the name implies, this fish comes from the Cichlidae family and is an aggressive territorial fish that will eat anything and everything. This ten-inch species can be mixed only with species that can take care of themselves.

(?)

Have you ever met a person like the Red Devil fish? The name itself brings up a red flag to me. These people are very territorial, very aggressive and enjoy confrontation. They are extremely argumentative and always right. It is their way or the highway. They have a difficult time embracing other people's ideas or suggestions and will shoot you down in a minute. As you are lying there wounded, they will go a step further and gobble you up. Have you ever worked for a person like that? Have you ever volunteered, perhaps in a church or for a non-profit organization, and worked under a person like that? Have you ever been guilty of acting like a Red Devil fish? Are you currently acting like a Red Devil fish? Does it bother you that you act like a Red Devil fish? If so, you can be delivered from this and know that help is on the way.

My mother was blessed with five children. Yes, I said blessed. The Bible teaches us children are a blessing from God. Some of you may not agree that children are a blessing. I believe they are. My mother refused to allow us to have pets. She said cleaning up after five children was enough. She did agree to us having fresh water fish. She purchased the bowl and fish. We were ecstatic.

Every day we would go downstairs in our family room and watch the fish. One day we realized that some of the fish were missing. We told Mom and she was puzzled, too. After a few days we came to realize the fish were being eaten by one of the bigger fish. At the time we had no idea what type of fish were in the bowl. My mother decided to handle this the "Frances" way. Please know that my mother is a woman of great wisdom. She has been married for 50 years. Any woman who has been married for fifty years has to have *some* wisdom.

She decided to put the culprit in a bowl by himself for a couple of days. Her thought was he would learn his lesson if she isolated him from interacting with the other fish. After a couple of days she put him back in the bowl with the other fish. The very next day we ran down the stairs to check on the fish and to our dismay all of the fish were gone except one. My mother was furious and decided to teach this fish a lesson. He went to a place where he could swim forever all by himself.

Some of you may be thinking or saying to yourselves you wish you could teach these "red devil" humans a lesson. You'd love to isolate them. However, there are laws that protect red devil humans. Legally you cannot take people out just because they act like a Red Devil fish. However, there are other positive things you can do. One of them is to try not to look at the behavior and look at why the person acts the way he or she does. I'm a firm believer that people do not get up in the morning and say, "Let me be a pain to someone today," or "I'm going to make it a point today to annoy everyone who comes in contact with me."

I believe there is a reason behind why people act the way they act. One of the biggest reasons is insecurity and fear. You would be surprised to know that some of the most accomplished, educated, intelligent and outgoing people have some real issues with being insecure. Due to the nature of my work and my involvement with people from many walks of life I've experienced these type of people time and time again. Once we overlook the behavior and try to understand perhaps why this person is acting this way, we have won half the battle.

Years ago earlier in my career I knew a person like this. I had a co-worker who had every characteristic of a Red Devil fish. Initially, I fought back with him every chance I got. He ended up becoming my manager and after that it got worse. He tried many times to eat me alive. Every time he attempted to attack me I came back with my own ammunition. After awhile I decided to try another approach. I said to myself, "This person has some real issues. I need to stop fighting and start loving." I noticed that this man was not a happy person. He always appeared sad. It was around Christmas and everyone was talking about spending time with family and friends. I asked him what he was going to do for the holiday and he said nothing. It bothered me so much that I decided to bake him some cookies. The next day, the last day before our time off for the holiday, I went to his office and gave him two-dozen homemade chocolate chip cookies. His eyes got as big as saucers as he tried to hold back the tears. He began to share with me some of his life experiences that were quite unpleasant. That was the beginning of a wonderful work relationship. I didn't have to teach him a lesson. I killed that red devil behavior with kindness.

It takes a lot to come to that point because most of us have been taught to fight back when attacked. However, the spiritual side of us teaches us to forgive, love and nurture. If you are acting like a Red Devil fish you can be freed from that behavior. All you have to do is call out for help. You don't have to verbally call out. You can inwardly ask for help. If you are sincere I know that someone will come in your path to assist you. It is a sad thing to float about in life acting like a Red Devil fish.

If you are a victim of a Red Devil fish try to be more understanding. After all, we all have flaws and none of us is perfect. People who act like Red Devil fish need love, too. That could be one of the reasons for their behavior. They weren't loved. Many people among us have been abused, used and mistreated. By the way, we did get another bowl of fish and never had the problem again.

Let's float on. Another type of fish is the Guppy. The Guppie or Rainbow fish is a small freshwater fish of South America and the West Indies. The guppy is named after the Rev. J.L. Guppy of Trinidad, an early collector of the species from the late 1800s. Guppies are in the same family as mollies and mosquito fish. The wild, original guppy is native to Central America, as well as Trinidad and northern South America. Today, many guppies are found in Asia, especially Singapore, where many fancy strains are bred in large fish farms and shipped to pet stores all over the world. The fancy guppies are the result of specialized breeding techniques and they only slightly resemble the small, wild guppy, often seen in pet stores labeled "feeder fish." Credit is due these active little fish, which are a joy for many who keep them. The guppy is a definite favorite because it is a very hardy fish that gives birth every month. The male is very colorful with a decorative tail and fins. However, the females are dull in color. These fish are considered a peaceful fish as opposed to being aggressive. They are very popular and showy.

(?)

Have you ever met a showy person? They are the life of the party. Some of you may remember the song "Track of My Tears" by Smokey Robinson.

These people always have to be up front. It is what I call "grinning and skinning." They are quick to come forth when they know they have an opportunity to be out front. They can fool you at times because they sometimes will give you the impression they don't like to be up front when in reality they do. It is very hard for them to give someone else a chance. They don't like to work behind the scenes because they like to be seen. They can appear to be peaceful people who don't like confrontation. They like everyone to like them. They have a problem when someone doesn't like them or doesn't agree with them.

I learned a long time ago there would be times when a person just doesn't like a person for no reason at all. I have run into situations when someone didn't like me and couldn't even tell me why. It is nice to be liked; however, if someone doesn't care for us its best to chalk it up and move on. There is no sense in wasting time trying to make someone like you. Life is too short and time is too precious a commodity. These guppy-type people also have a hard time delegating. If they do delegate, they stay right on top of you. This makes a person feel as though they are suffocating. They also fall in the category of perfectionist. Everything has to be just right. These guppy-type people may appear to be very secure, but inwardly they are the opposite. I know about these guppy-type people because I have been guilty of having some of the characteristics of a guppy. I used to have a difficult time delegating. I often tell people that I am a reformed perfectionist. Over the years I've worked at learning how to delegate and trust others. I used to think the only way something was going to get done was to do it myself. Today, I still have to work on that. Sometimes you have to turn things over to people and allow them to make mistakes. Many times I didn't turn things over to others because I didn't trust them. Many people have been instrumental in my life. These special people gave me an opportunity to grow by delegating responsibility to me. When I began to give that some thought I quickly came to realize that I too had to let go and allow others to excel in what they were put on Earth to do. I never want to hinder someone else's growth or hamstring a person from walking into his or her destiny. I'd like to be known as the person who was instrumental in empowering someone to reach his or her destiny. That is why I take what I do seriously. I serve others by assisting them in reaching their fullest potential.

If you have the characteristics of a guppy, don't be afraid to get out of the limelight for a minute and take some time to reflect. If you really are supposed to be up-front, then by all means stay there! However, remain there in the right spirit and with the right motives. Sometimes we fail to do what we should be doing because we are so busy doing the wrong things. We get so preoccupied with "busyness" we can't see our way out. I know people who are very visible publicly, but inwardly their hurts and cries for help remain undetected. When those individuals have come to me for advice I prayerfully listen to them. Many times I never have to say a word. I just give them the space and time to pour out their feelings. Often they end up talking themselves right where they desire to be and at that time are willing to do whatever needs to be done to get there.

The last fish I'd like to talk about is the Kissing Gourami or Pink Kisser or Green Kissing Gourami.

This fish comes from Thailand, Malaysia, Borneo and Sumatra. Generally, this fish is oval in shape when looked at from the side. From the front it appears very thin and compressed. In younger fish the forehead area is dimpled. Perhaps it is best known for its thick lips, which protrude when the fish is grazing algae. The so-called kissing behavior is not affection but a form of challenge, probably related to reproduction. The dorsal and anal fins start at the front of the body and go back to the start of the tail fin. The tail fin is somewhat concave in shape.

The basic background color of the Pink Kisser is a pale pink. There are no other distinguishing color variations that can easily be seen. The Pink Kisser is just a variety of the Green Kissing Gourami. The Green Kissers' body is a shiny green, interlaced with dark reddish, horizontal stripes. Two short vertical bars run across the gill covers. The fins are a pale green to gray in color.

All these fish do is float around in the tank or bowl kissing anything and every-thing they can get their lips on. Of course, these fish are considered peaceful.

(?)

Do you have characteristics of a Kissing fish? Do you know people like that? These people will kiss up to any and everything just to get what they want.

However, when it is all said and done these people are usually disappointed. At some point they realize after they've obtained their goal it wasn't worth what they gave up to get it. I've spoken with people who have experienced this. They begin to feel worthless, cheated and used. These people are very difficult to work with in a team setting. They don't have a mind of their own and they will agree with the leader just to score brownie points. Other team members do not trust them and as a result they hold back from contributing, while others smack the kissing fish in the face and proceed to give their input. Have you been in settings like this? I have and it can be quite frustrating. However, a good leader will recognize what is going on and will attempt to manage the team in a way that is effective. In my mind that is one of the characteristics of a good leader. A good leader is able to work with others from diverse backgrounds, skill sets and behaviors and successfully excel in accomplishing goals and objectives. It takes patience, prayer, time, humbleness, heartaches and a number of good and bad experiences to be an effective leader. Note that I did not say a leader—I said an *effective* leader.

Some of you may be drowning right now. The water has really come over the deck and attacked you ferociously. Some of you may see yourself in more than one fish that has been described. You may be thinking this was supposed to be an enjoyable, adventuresome cruise. You may be crying out for this to end. You've had enough. If that is you, my mission has been accomplished thus far. Don't jump ship! Continue the reading.

Sometimes we have to experience pain before we gain. The pain in this is coming to a place where you recognize that this is not a healthy way to live. You may have already acknowledged that something has to change and are now willing to do whatever needs to be done to live victoriously. You may be thinking, this hurts, there has to be a better way. There is a better way. The Bible states the devil, (not the Red Devil fish) "…the devil, comes to steal, kill and destroy, but Jesus came so that we can have life and have it more abundantly." *(John 10:10)*. According to Merriam-Webster's Online Dictionary the word abundance means "a relative degree of plentifulness." There are many people who are living abundant lives. I'm not talking about abundance from just a material perspective. I'm talking about abundance materially and inwardly. Many people have a wealth of money along with material possessions but inwardly they are a wreck. They have no inner peace and have a hard time trusting others. I've also met people who have no material abundance and they are a wreck also. One is just as bad as the other.

I strongly believe that our Creator is concerned about all aspects of our lives, including the spiritual, the emotional, the physical, the financial, and the relational. That is why the passage says, "…I have come to give you abundant life," abundance as it relates to your relationships, abundance as it relates to your finances, abundance as it relates to your spirituality and abundance as it relates to your emotions.

When you float through life and do not address issues that relate to your character you will continually bump into situations that are painful and harmful. You will never find any real satisfaction or contentment. Some of us float through life with many accomplishments and successes and still have no peace or sense of contentment. Have you ever stopped to take the time to realize that although you are successful you still have not fulfilled the purpose of your life here on Earth?

So ask yourself these questions: "What is success?" "Am I really successful if I'm not doing what I've been put on Earth to do?" When you are doing what you were put here to do, there is an inexplicable inner-peace resonating within that can take you through any adverse situation that may come your way. It may appear on the outside that your life is chaotic. However, inwardly, the peace that surpasses all understanding will keep you focused and fixed on the goal that must be accomplished.

No man is an island. Believe it or not we need each other and we also need peace and joy in our lives. It is a sad feeling to go through life wandering and never accomplishing what we were really put here to do. How many times have we experienced storms in our lives that drive us from side to side like the swaying of the trees? We begin to cry out but our pleas are to the wrong person or, frustrated, we attempt to fix it ourselves.

A real friend will tell you about yourself regardless of how you may take it. As you are reading this book those of you who have never met me know that I am an unseen friend. I know that some of this hurts. That is what real friends do; they're painfully honest with you because they care. I have had some painful experiences with people who got upset with me because I did not agree with decisions they made. The statement was as follows:

"If you really were my friend you would agree with me regardless and support me."

My response remains the same:

"I am your friend, I will accept your decision, but I cannot support it because I don't agree with it. It doesn't sit right with me. If I am wrong then time will tell and if I'm correct and it doesn't work out for you I'll be right here." I have lost so-called friendships over that response. However, the good news is those same people ended up coming back. I have found that you have to be honest with people even if it means ruffling them up a little. I'd rather lose a friendship than be responsible for someone never reaching his or her goal in life and remaining miserable. By the way, this also holds true for dealing with family members.

Most people have good intentions. Most people reach out and try to assist others as they go through seasons in their lives. All of this is admirable. However, when it is done in our own strength as opposed to being led by the Creator, the long-term results are always much more effective. Over the last fifteen years I have had the awesome privilege of teaching adults practical spiritual truths applicable to their lives. These truths have been passed on to their offspring or those in their circle of influence (family, friends, associates, co-workers, etc.) with the cycle continuing throughout generations. All of my input or contribution is not me, myself and I. It was led by my Creator who is far more intelligent than I. In other words, I have been used as an instrument. It has never been me and me alone. I take no credit. I'm just grateful that I have been called and chosen to do this good work.

Many of us face challenges when we look for answers to questions regarding our livelihood. Once the answer has been revealed, if the answer doesn't line up with what is acceptable in our minds, many times we immediately reject it and go back to doing it our own way. We come out of prayer, counsel or mediation and do our own thing and, when it fails, we find ourselves putting the blame on others instead of acknowledging perhaps we were just wrong. We missed it. We fell short.

Are you tired of floating around? Do you want to work on developing your character by getting rid of those characteristics in the Red Devil, Guppy and Kissing fish? Are you willing to help others who have those characteristics? If you answered, "Yes" to any of these questions you've taken a big step in getting set free. Did you know that as you help others in turn it brings freedom to you? There is nothing more gratifying that helping someone else.

3

SHIPWRECK

According to Webster's Dictionary "shipwreck" means:

a.   the remains of a wrecked ship.

b.   any ruin or destruction.

Most of us are quite familiar with the nursery rhyme Humpty Dumpty. Allow me to revisit this nursery rhyme and then expound on it.

Humpty Dumpty sat on a wall
Humpty Dumpty had a GREAT fall
All the King's horses and all the King's men couldn't put Humpty together again.

Let's take this rhyme line by line and dissect it.

Humpty Dumpty sat on a wall.

It does not say that Humpty Dumpty was "sitting on a wall". It says he "sat" on a wall, which leads me to believe that he was on that wall for quite some time. How long?
I have no idea, but long enough to do some damage to himself internally.

What was Humpty sitting on? He was sitting on a wall.

What does a wall represent? It represents a barrier, a shield, something that divides.

Humpty most likely got tired of all the drama in his life and decided to park himself on the wall he built. Perhaps Humpty was tired of all the drama at work, dealing with the kids, dealing with the spouse, dealing with church folk, dealing with in-laws, family and friends.

Does this sound familiar?

How many of us have been or are currently at the same place in life as Humpty? You're tired of being hurt, abused, misused, and feeling as though you are a victim, tired of being misunderstood, harassed, confused and perplexed. You're just tired of BEING!!!!

As a result, you have built up walls to keep everyone OUT including those who can help. The walls have begun to encircle around you. You have become so comfortable that you have decided to take a seat right on top of the wall and park yourself there for eternity.

I believe Humpty said, "Forget this. I'm going to take this into my own hands. I've had it. I know exactly what I'm going to do. I'm going to build these walls of protection around myself so no one and nothing can penetrate them. I'm going to take care of this situation once and for all. I'm going to escape from all this mess and float myself into my own world and stay right up here on this wall and I dare anyone to try to get me to come down. I dare you. I double dare you".

(?)

Does this sound familiar? Have you been there? Do you know of anyone who has been there? I've been there and believe me it isn't a good place.

What is significant about this are the words I, I've or I'm. In that short passage of words it is used ten times.

What I am going to do.

I'm going to take care of this.

Old Humpty was saying, "I'm going to float my own boat".

"I'm the captain of this ship".

Old Humpty continued building this wall and all of a sudden he had a

GREAT FALL—SHIPWRECK!!

Old Humpty sank.

This is what happens when we take matters into our own hands. We usually end up
SHIPWRECKED!!

Let's continue.

All the king's horses and all the king's men couldn't put Humpty together again. Old Humpty was broken, shattered and confused. He physically came apart. Guess what? He was emotionally shattered and shipwrecked way before the fall. The fall was just a public demonstration of what was happening inwardly.

(?)

Do you feel as though you are about to shipwreck?
Do you know anyone who is about to shipwreck?

If you haven't shipwrecked yet, you don't want to go there.
You don't want anyone you know to shipwreck.
Pull those oars back and allow yourself to be redirected.

Are you already there?

If the answer is "Yes", I have GREAT NEWS; you can get OUT!

I've been there. I've gotten out and don't want to go back there again.

Let's continue to cruise.

Everyone tried to pick up the broken pieces of a shattered life. However, no one was able to put Humpty back together again.

Do you know why?

SHIPWRECK

No one really knew Humpty. No one was intimate with him. No one had an understanding about Humpty. No one took the time out to learn Humpty and no one was wise about Humpty. Remember the definition for the words "knowing" and "knew"?
The only person who knew Humpty was the one who created him. Sometimes we think we know ourselves, but let me remind you that you did not create yourself. In order to get to know yourself you must know your Creator.

Now the story of Humpty Dumpty ended right there. However, your story does not have to end there unless you choose to end it there.

Allow me to give you another rendition of Humpty Dumpty as I attempt to cruise into this next port. I attribute this wonderful rendition of Humpty Dumpty to David Baroni.

Humpty Dumpty sat on a wall
Humpty Dumpty had such a terrible fall that
All the king's horses and all the king's men
Couldn't help ole Humpty get it together again
With his life all in pieces he did the right thing
In the depths of his dilemma he called on the King
Then the King said, "Humpty, I've been watching you.
Just waiting for this chance to pull you through."

Humpty Dumpty's back together again
And he's happier now than he's ever been
Found his purpose for living, his old life's forgiven
Made old Humpty Dumpty better than new!

Is this story familiar? Could ole Humpty be you?
And tho' you've tried all of the answers, still you're coming unglued.
Why don't you call on the King instead of horses and men?
You'll be amazed at the change as the miracle begins, oh!

You see life can work much better than a nursery rhyme
Cause there's a God, who really loves you,
And he promised to be with you all of the time.

Once upon a time ole Humpty was me,
Then the King came along and He made me complete.
And Jesus still makes me complete.

Humpty Dumpty's back together again,
And I'm happier now than I've ever been.
Found my purpose for living, my old life's forgiven,
King Jesus came to my rescue,
Made this Humpty better than new,
And He'll do the same for you.
Are you a Humpty Dumpty too?

David Baroni
Copyright 1989 Pleasant Hill Music/BMI
Used with permission

All the king's horses and all the king's men couldn't put Humpty together again. They were most likely well-meaning people who were trying to put Humpty back together in their own strength and it was not working. Again, when you try to float your boat in your own power and strength or in someone else's you will eventually shipwreck. Remember, you can shipwreck inwardly and no one will ever know. Be mindful that shipwrecking is not just a public demonstration.

Many on the outside appear to have it all: money, power, fine homes, cars and all the luxuries this world can give. However, inwardly they are shipwrecked. There is no peace, no real joy; they don't even know whom they can trust. I've heard some say they'd rather have it all and be inwardly distraught as opposed to not having anything and still be inwardly distraught.

My perspective is, I'd rather have it all and not be inwardly distraught or ship-wrecked, and YOU CAN!! "The blessing of the Lord makes one rich and he adds no sorrow with it." (*Proverbs 10:22*).

(?)

Are you tired of bumping around and shipwrecking?

Are you tired of being misled and confused?

Are you tired of living up to someone else's expectations?

WHAT IS MORE IMPORTANT?

To be liked or to like yourself?

To complain or be thankful?

To always be on the receiving end or to be a giver?

To learn from your mistakes or ignore the lessons to be learned?

To blame others for your mistakes or take a good look at your own actions?

To admit you need help in certain areas of your life or camouflage it, suppress it and stay internally locked up in prison?

Are you willing to let go of your ways, your ideas, and your thoughts and allow the presence of the Creator consume your life and take you on a journey that is life-changing, rewarding and gratifying?

Are you ready to feast at a table that never runs out of food? This table is far better than any midnight buffet on any cruise ship.

This food consists of:

- love
- joy
- peace
- patience
- kindness
- goodness
- faithfulness
- gentleness

- and self-control

This food is not tangible. This food is not for sale. It is just like the Master Card: It is priceless.

4

YOUR BOAT

(?)

Is your boat equipped to sail smoothly?

In other words, what condition are you in?

Do you find yourself wandering without focus or direction?

Do you find yourself existing here on Earth with no fulfillment?

Do you find yourself not physically, mentally or spiritually fit to deal with life?

Do you find yourself wondering if there is more to life than what you are experiencing?

Let's take a look at a well-equipped boat. Various components make up a boat. Allow me to take a moment to expound on a few that are crucial for a successful voyage.

Anchor—An anchor is a heavy metal object designed so that its weight and shape will help to hold a boat in its position when lowered to the bottom of the sea.

Ballast—A ballast is a weight at the bottom of the boat to help keep it stable.

Bow—A bow is the forward part of the boat, the boat's <u>face.</u>

Bridge—The bridge is the area from which a ship is controlled. The location from which a vessel or boat is steered and its speed controlled. The bridge is known as the cockpit on a smaller boat. The boat's <u>brain.</u>

Hull—The hull is the main structural body of the boat, not including the deck, keel, mast, or cabin. It is the part that keeps the water out of the boat. The main body of the boat.
The <u>immune system</u> of the boat.

Keel—A keel is a flat surface built into the bottom of the boat to prevent or reduce the leeway caused by the wind pushing against the side of the boat. The <u>back</u> of the boat.

Porthole—A porthole is a window in the side of a boat, usually round or with rounded corners. Sometimes portholes can be opened; sometimes they are fixed shut. The <u>eyes</u> of the boat.

In life we go through seasons. We have seasons of joy and seasons of pain. During the seasons of pain we are sometimes lowered to the bottom. However, just because we hit hard times does not mean we cannot be lifted again. If you are anchored, "correctly" you can still maintain and hold your position and eventually come out of it. When you are at the bottom there are a couple of choices that you can make: You can remain there or come out of it. When we are not anchored "correctly" or our anchor is misplaced we find ourselves staying at the bottom of the sea and making excuses, like blaming others or even blaming ourselves.

(?)

Are you anchored? In other words, what are you anchored in?

In order for a boat to have a successful voyage all of its parts must be in working order. In the case of a disaster, it is crucial that the anchor is functional. In order for us as humans to have a successful victorious journey our anchor should be one that can sustain, support and withstand the test of time. It should be functional also. The key here is to make sure we are *properly* anchored. Many of us anchor ourselves in other people. We anchor ourselves in our jobs, in our spouses, in our money, in our children and even in ourselves. Then when these anchors fail us—such as losing a job, our children disappointing us or our spouses fail to meet all of our expectations—we fall apart. There is no person on the face of this Earth that can meet all of our needs or expectations. Many times we set people up when we make promises. They expect us to deliver, and when we are not able it causes hurt, resentment, pain and oftentimes bitterness.

My anchor happens to be my Creator. That is the only safe place where I can anchor myself. When all hell breaks loose and nothing else seems to work that is when I take solace in knowing I am anchored in my Creator. I know that if I end up at the bottom of the sea for whatever reason I will come out because my anchor, my Creator, has the power, the might and "know all" to get me out of anything. I also know that if I allow my Creator to guide and lead I can avoid some shipwrecks.

Let's take a look at the human body. There are various components that are needed in order for humans to physically sail through life successfully.

The human body is the most fascinating and artistic creation in existence. No human can fully understand all of its mysteries; and no single source can do justice to its many parts. The human body is comprised of many different parts such as the feet, hands, neck and stomach just to name a few. More than half of the bones in the human body are in the hands and feet. Tendons connect the muscles that act on the various bones of the toes and feet to help us stand and walk. The bones of the fingers and thumb are jointed to the palm, which is jointed to eight bones that make up our wrist which subsequently, become jointed to the two arm bones that support our hands. The function of the stomach is best described as a food processing unit and a storage device. It looks like a defeated balloon when empty, but when full it becomes about a foot long and six inches wide and is able to hold about two quarts of food and drink. The stomach is both chemical and mechanical. Chemicals like the digestive enzymes, pepsin, rennin, and lipase interact to breakdown food. The mechanical action of the muscles in the stomach constrict and relax in a continuous motion blending substances together so they can be processed by the small intestine.

The ear is the part of the body that contains the sensory organs of hearing and balance. The ear can be divided into three parts. The external ear serves to protect the membranes and capture sound. The middle ear transmits and amplifies sound waves. The inner ear functions to convert mechanical energy transferred by the middle ear into neural impulses.

The neck contains important communication between the head and the body, including air and food passages, major blood vessels, nerves and the spinal cord. When humans eat food, it must first go through the neck in order to begin the breakdown process on its way to the stomach. The neck also houses the larynx or voice box by which we use to speak. The backbone or spinal column is a flexible structure made of twenty-six bones. The backbone provides structure from which all other upper body structures branch, and it protects the spinal nerve. It also serves as the highway for all the information your brain sends as your body travels. The backbone is approximately twenty-eight inches long. The gallbladder and pancreas lie outside of the gastrointestinal tract. The pancreas is a producer of digestive enzymes. The gallbladder is a small reservoir for bile. The liver reproduces nutrients so they can be used for cell rebuilding or energy. The teeth are gears to demolish chunks of food. They do the first drastic destruction to food in the digestive system. The tongue helps to remove and dislocate food particles in the teeth and shifts food around in the mouth in order to assist with swallowing. The skull is the most important structure in the skeletal system. The skull provides the framework for the sensory organs such as eyes, ears, tongue and nose. The skull also houses the brain.

The human body although simple in some areas and complex in others should be well taken care of and protected. If severely damaged in any way, the results could be life threatening. We need our bodies to be healthy if we are to fulfill all that we were put here on Earth to do. There is a passage that says "Beloved, I wish among all things that you would prosper and be in good health even as your soul prospers." (3rd John 2).

When our bodies are in good health we can enjoy life. It is very sad to see people who are so unhealthy physically they are unable to enjoy life. What's the point in working hard all your life, neglecting your body then retiring after all of those years of hard work to suffer because your body is broken down? No amount of money in the world can fix a shipwrecked body. There are times when money can delay disaster. However, many people end up leaving this world sooner because of failing to maintain a healthy body. Take care of your body, it's the only one you have.

(?)

If your boat is equipped to sail smoothly, then ask yourself this question:

Why have I not sailed as smoothly as I'd like?

If your boat is not equipped to sail smoothly, help is on the way. There is a resolution to your dilemma.

Man is not body only. We also have a spirit and a body. Thus, the wholeness of man includes:

- mind

- body (human anatomy)

- and spirit

However, many of us tend to focus on a healthy physical body and neglect the other two. Some focus on the spirit only and neglect the other two. Others focus on the mind and neglect the others. In order to sail through life successfully we must embrace all three: the mind, the body and the spirit. Most of us came into this world with a sound mind. I admonish you to protect and safeguard your mind, your thoughts and your emotions. If you don't have a sound mind it is nearly impossible to be productive in this life.

Let's dive deeper into the ocean, go underneath and further examine what it takes to be whole and sail through life. I trust you will be enlightened. Your body houses your spirit. It is very important that your spirit is awakened. The awakening of your spirit is referred to as being "born again" or "spiritually renewed". A new birth has taken place when your spirit is awakened. It is not a natural birth such as coming out of a womb. It is a spiritual birth. Once that spiritual birth takes place you will begin to see life in a different way. When your spirit lies dormant or is never awakened you end up going through life missing an element that is crucial to your well-being. You end up being crippled. It's like functioning without some of your major body parts. It is much easier to get through life with all your parts functioning well. That is most likely why some of you are wondering what is missing in your life. I've been there. About 20 years ago I asked myself that same question. What is missing in my life? Intellectually (mind) and physically (body) you may have it all together. However, you may be feeling empty or tired. The missing link—your spirituality or an inactive spirit. In order for your boat to float effectively and go in the direction where you will find true fulfillment you must grasp and embrace the missing link, your spirituality.

(?)

1). Do I see where I have missed the boat?

2). Do I see it and don't want to address it?

3). Do I see it and want to address it so I can move on and be the victorious person that I was destined to be in all areas of my life?

Regardless of how you answered the above questions let's sail on.

In order for a boat to sail smoothly, all of its parts must be working in order. The same is true with our human body. When one of our parts is not working properly it affects other areas of our body. This is also true with our mind, body and spirit.

If all of them are not functioning correctly we find ourselves off-balance. If one area is dead, we find ourselves lacking. We find ourselves feeling as though something is missing. Many times we make sure our intellectual and physical needs are met and don't address our spirituality. Our spirituality remains dormant. As a result, we end up spiritually dying. You don't have to end up dying spiritually if you choose to allow your spirit to awaken. Once that spirituality is awakened you will begin to see things differently; you will begin to live. You will begin to thirst and hunger after those things that matter. You will begin to have a different perspective on life. You will begin to realize that your way may not be the best way and you will begin to humble yourself and sail on a different course. You will still dance and sing and celebrate and enjoy life but you will dance and sing and celebrate and enjoy life to a different drummer who happens to have an *awesome* beat.

Some of you may be wondering what you need to do in order for your spirit to be awakened. I'm so glad that thought crossed your mind. It is very simple. Some of you may have already made that decision, but find yourselves needing to make the commitment again. Take some time to read and meditate on the following and if you are in agreement go back and read the words out loud. If you're not in agreement continue the reading.

I've been like a ship that's tossed and driven; battered by the angry sea. The storms of life have been raging and the fury has fallen on me. I wonder what I have done that makes this race in life so hard to run. I say to myself, "take courage" and know the Lord will make a way for me somehow.

I now ask the Creator and the Lord Jesus to forgive me for my past mistakes and I make a decision to pull in this oar, bow beneath the Creator and allow him to take away my burdens, pain, confusion, emptiness and hurt. I no longer want to drift through life. I desire to have a fulfilling life with meaning and purpose. I no longer want to live my life through others. I want to be the person that I was put on this Earth to be.
I realize that by anchoring myself in someone who is higher than I, I can find peace and clear direction in all that I do. I'm not sure how all of this is going to work out but I am willing to dock this boat, get out and walk in a different direction.
In other words, I'm making a decision to surrender my life to the will of God—my Creator. I recognize that only through the one who created me can I find real contentment, peace and inner prosperity.

You are never too old, never too educated, never too successful, never too rich, never too young and never too poor to turn your life around for the better.

Read the above again and again. Read it to yourself. Read it out loud. Allow it to sink in. Trust me. You will not shipwreck this time.

5

MY BOAT

I was like that ship that was tossed and driven.

In December of 1985 it was time for me to get out of the boat (out of my comfort zone). I decided to sail in another direction. I was in graduate school, studying in Atlanta, Georgia. I had a select group of friends that I hung out with. I also had a car to drive. I had a roof over my head, plenty of food to eat and clothes to put on my back. I was on my way to fulfilling one of my goals. In the eyes of many I was blessed. However, deep inside there was no contentment. I was raised in the church, but I never had a personal relationship with God. I was just *there*.

I was living in a home with a man and woman who had personal relationships with God (Ralph and Susie Norwood). They were humble people who took in others. They were never forceful or rude and they both loved me unconditionally. They were very patient with me. They recognized that I enjoyed reading and began giving me a variety of books. I began to read inspirational/spiritual books and began to study Christianity. I spent hours and hours digging, researching and studying along with the school workload in my graduate program.

One evening while studying in my room I made the decision to embrace the element in my life that had been missing—the spirit. I was not at a church or attending a church event. However, the presence of God was there. It was me and my Creator and my Creator and me. It was absolutely *awesome*. Words cannot fully describe that moment. This was a very special moment for me and one that I will never forget. I spoke words that were similar to those that you read above.

From that point on my life took on a new meaning and I've enjoyed an adventuresome, fulfilling life. Prior to that I had only exercised the mind and the body. But in December of 1985 I made a commitment to allow the spirit of God to come into my life and to be my tour guide and the captain of this ship. It has worked for me over the last 20 years and it can work for you, too. It has not always been smooth sailing. I've had many disappointments. However, when it is all said and done I'm still standing and I'm whole. In addition, I've been helping others for the last fifteen years. What a life this has been! What an abundant life! You, too, can have that life. God sent his Son to this Earth for all of us and his desire is for all of us to have fulfillment in all areas of our lives. God does not have favorites. He loves us all.

As I was sitting on the beach in Cancun summer before last, early in the morning taking in God's creation and watching the waves fold and unfold, I experienced something that was breathtaking and unforgettable. As the waves continued to fold and unfold every now and then the sun appeared and then disappeared. This scene reminded me of the Son of God who appears in our lives as the waves fold and unfold. Often times we don't recognize that he is there and he hides himself but never leaves. As the waves of life fold and unfold he re-appears and re-appears and then SUDDENLY we realize that the SON is here and that he is not going anywhere.

That time on the beach reminded me of the song titled "Here Comes the Sun". One of the song's lyrics says, "Here comes the sun that makes my life worth living again." My version of this song is exactly what it says. I just change the word Sun to Son. The Son of my Creator who came to this Earth and as a result, my life is worth living.

Was it easy for me to make the transition? No.

Was it painful? Yes.

It was not easy for me to make the transition because of the environment I was in at that time. The challenge I faced was the graduate program. It was developed with a team concept. As a result, I still had to mingle with the team. This team of people happened to be my friends. My friends had other interests, and although they respected my decision they were not interested in the decision that I made at that time. As a result, I had to limit my interactions with them. It was very painful for me because I felt so alone. Even though I was feeling alone; I was not alone. God had already taken care of that.

The woman of the house I was living in (Susie Norwood, whom we affectionately called "Ma Dear") took me under her wings for a year and a half. She nurtured, encouraged and stood by me throughout the remainder of my tenure at graduate school. This is one of the reasons why I have such compassion for people who struggle with making the transition from non-spirituality to spirituality. Some-one was there for me and I vowed that I would someday be able to reciprocate. My desire came true. Since 1989 I have assisted others in making that transition through teaching, admonishing and supporting. It has been absolutely gratifying and rewarding. There is nothing more gratifying than seeing lives changed for the better. You cannot put a price on that.

Do I regret it?

I have never regretted the decision that I made years ago to allow my Creator to be the captain of my ship. It has been a wonderful adventure and I have been truly blessed professionally, spiritually, financially, emotionally and physically. I can honestly tell you that our Creator does not miss a beat. It has not been a cake-walk nor has it been a bed of roses at all times. It has built character, discipline and humility. If you have chosen to make the decision I did, I assure you—you will not regret it.

6

TIME TO GET OFF THE BOAT

Thank you for going on this journey with me. Now it is time to get off the boat, put your feet on dry land and go forward. Going forward is going to be a process. Now is the time to activate. In other words, put into action what you've gotten out of this reading.

It's one thing to turn on the car; it is another to put your foot on the pedal.

It's one thing to put the worm on the hook; it is another to toss the bait in the water.

It's one thing to pray or mediate; it is another to accept the answer, especially when the answer is not what you expect.

Will you continue to let other others chart your course? Will you continue to float yourself or will you make the choice to allow the Creator to be the captain of your ship? The choice is yours. As you begin to make your exit off the boat and plant your feet firmly on land, my desire for you is that all burdens have been lifted. The anxiety, confusion and turmoil have been tossed overboard and are forever lost in the sea. That is exactly what happens when you throw up your hands and allow the Creator to come in. He forgives you for everything and anything you have done and throws it into the sea of forgiveness. The nice thing about it is he doesn't ever bring it back up. Others may, but he doesn't. The most important thing for you to do at this point is to forgive yourself. We are our biggest critics. None of us are perfect. However, we are forgiven. You are now ready to begin to move forward without the trunks. What really matters when it is all said and done is that you fulfilled the plan for your life ordained for you before the foundations of the Earth.

Allow me to offer some brief advice as you step out and move forward.

- Be teachable
- Be open
- Be honest

These are key ingredients to success. Many times we don't allow others to assist us. My prayer for you is that the right person or people will come in your path to help you along the way. Once that occurs, I pray that you will be open, transparent and honest. I also pray that you will be alert to anybody or anything that hinders you from fulfilling your destiny. In order for you to grow spiritually you need to be in an environment that promotes healthy spiritual/biblical, practical and wholesome teaching that addresses the mind, body and spirit.

You need to surround yourself with positive people who will address all areas of your life and show you how to practically incorporate spiritual and biblical truths into your everyday life. Stay AWAY from negative people and complainers. My prayer for you is that you will be led to that place and/or to those people.

It is my desire that you will not shipwreck as you venture out. If you do not know where to go as it relates to getting a solid foundation I will be happy to assist you.

I can be contacted at:

www.wfybsite.com

or

dfareed@wfybsite.com

I trust the next time you hear the phrase "Whatever Floats Your Boat" or you feel like saying "Whatever Floats Your Boat" it will have new meaning.

APPENDIX

If you are interested in participating in an interactive "Whatever Floats Your Boat" workshop or if you are interested in hosting a workshop send an E-mail to:

dfareed@wfybsite.com and include the following:

Your Name:

Address:

City:

State:

Zip Code:

Phone:

E-mail Address:

OR

Complete and submit the form on the "Contact The Author" page at: **www.wfybsite.com**

OR

Contact us toll-free at **1-888-761-1808.**

AUTHOR BIOGRAPHY

Donna Fareed (Warfield) was born and raised in Rochester, New York. She is the wife of Mel Fareed and the daughter of Vern and Mary Frances Warfield. She is a graduate of Wilberforce University, Atlanta University and Spiritual Life Training Center. She also attended Oral Roberts University.

The author's diverse background includes teaching, facilitating, consulting, program management, and sales/marketing. In addition to being an Adjunct Faculty Professor, she has enjoyed a career in Information Technology for the last 22 years. Donna sits on the Board of Directors as Technology Chair for the Georgia Association of Personnel Services (GAPS).

Over the last 15 years, Donna has been very active teaching specifically in the area of discipleship. She is a sought after Bible teacher and inspirational speaker and has also served as a short-term missionary to Africa.

As a child, the author was always an avid reader and writer. While in elementary school, she read every Bobbsey Twin book in the school library by renowned author, Laura Lee Hope. As an adult, her passion for reading and writing remained with her as she has written curriculum, manuals, and articles, for churches, businesses and associations throughout the United States.

0-595-34203-5

Printed in the United States
31454LVS00001B/118-225